The Origin of Evil

By Helena P. Blavatsky

Copyright © 2021 Lamp of Trismegistus. All rights reserved. No part of this publication may be reproduced or transmitted in any form or by any means, electronic or mechanical, including photocopying, recording, or by any information storage and retrieval system, without permission in writing from Lamp of Trismegistus. Reviewers may quote brief passages.

ISBN: 978-1-63118-581-6

Esoteric Classics

Other Books in this Series and Related Titles

Aurora of the Philosophers by Paracelsus (978-1-63118-507-6)

Clairvoyance and Psychic Abilities by A Besant &c (978-1-63118-403-1)

The Feminine Occult by various authors (978-1-63118-711-7)

Rosicrucian Rules, Secret Signs, Codes and Symbols by various (978-1-63118-488-8)

An Outline of Theosophy by C W Leadbeater (978-1-63118-452-9)

Paracelsus, the Four Elements and Their Spirits by M P Hall (978-1-63118-400-0)

Essays on Ancient Magic by Helena P Blavatsky (978-1-63118-535-9)

Essays on the Esoteric Tradition of Karma by A Besant &c (978-1-63118-426-0)

The Use of Evil by Annie Besant (978-1-63118-532-8)

Occult Arts by William Q. Judge (978-1-63118-559-5)

The Alchemical Catechism of Paracelsus by Paracelsus (978-1-63118-513-7)

Alchemy in the Nineteenth Century by Helena P Blavatsky (978-1-63118-446-8)

Qabbalistic Teachings and the Tree of Life by M P Hall (978-1-63118-482-6)

The Historic, Mythic and Mystic Christ by Annie Besant (978–1–63118–533–5)

The Hidden Mysteries of Christianity by Annie Besant (978–1–63118–534–2)

History, Analysis and Secret Tradition of the Tarot by Hall &c (978-1-63118-445-1)

Kali the Mother by Sister Nivedita (978-1-63118-558-8)

Arcane Formulas or Mental Alchemy by W W Atkinson (978-1-63118-459-8)

The Machinery of the Mind by Dion Fortune (978-1-63118-451-2)

The A E Waite Reader: A Selection of Occult Essays (978-1-63118-515-1)

The Leadbeater Reader: A Selection of Occult Essays (978-1-63118-483-3)

Audio versions are also available on Audible, Amazon and Apple

Other Books in this Series and Related Titles

The Camp of Philosophy: Studies in Alchemy by Bloomfield (978–1–63118–580–9)

The Testaments of the Twelve Patriarchs (978–1–63118–579–3)

Occult or Exact Science? by Helena P Blavatsky (978–1–63118–578–6)

Occultism, Semi-Occultism & Pseudo Occultism by A Besant (978–1–63118–577–9)

The Fourth-Gospel and Synoptical Problem by G R S Mead (978–1–63118–576–2)

On the Bhagavad-Gita by T Subba Row &c (978–1–63118–575–5)

What Theosophy Does for Us by C W Leadbeater (978–1–63118–574–8)

Spiritual Life for Man by Annie Besant (978–1–63118–573–1)

The Mysteries by Annie Besant (978–1–63118–572–4)

Fundamental Ideas of Theosophy by Bhagwan Das (978–1–63118–571–7)

Dreams: What They Are and Caused by C W Leadbeater (978–1–63118–570–0)

Communication Between Different Worlds by Annie Besant (978–1–63118–569–4)

Animism, Magic and the Omnipotence of Thought by S Freud (978–1–63118–568–7)

Buddhism by F Otto Schrader (978–1–63118–567–0)

Death by W W Westcott (978–1–63118–566–3)

The Religion of Theosophy by Bhagwan Das (978–1–63118–565–6)

The Spirit of Zoroastrianism by Henry S Olcott (978–1–63118–564–9)

The Brotherhood of Religions by Annie Besant (978–1–63118–563–2)

Fourth Book of Maccabees by Josephus (978-1-63118-562-5)

The Story of Ahikar by Ahiqar (978-1-63118-561-8)

Vision of the Spirit by C. Jinarajadasa (978-1-63118-560-1)

Audio versions are also available on Audible, Amazon and Apple

Table of Contents

Introduction...7

The Origin of Evil...9

Stray Thoughts on Death and Satan
Edited by H. P. Blavatsky...27

I. Death by Eliphas Levi...31

II. Satan by Eliphas Levi...38

INTRODUCTION

The word "esoteric" can be difficult to define. Esotericism in general can be seen less as a system of beliefs and more as a category, which encompasses numerous, different systems of beliefs. It's a bit of juxtaposition, since the word "esoteric" indicates something that few people know about, while the term itself broadly covers numerous philosophies, practices, areas of study and belief systems.

In a greater sense, Esotericism acts as a storehouse for secret knowledge, which is often considered ancient (by *tradition, if not by fact),* passed down from generation to generation, in private. At various times in history, simply possessing the knowledge of some of these subjects, was considered illegal and a jailable offence, if discovered. This usually included such general topics as Alchemy, Pharmacology, Qabalah, Hermeticism, Occultism, Ceremonial Magic, Astrology, Divination, Rosicrucianism and so on. Collectively, these areas of study were often referred to as the esoteric sciences.

Sometimes, the outer garment of a subject isn't esoteric, while what is hidden beneath it, is. As an example, Freemasonry isn't necessarily esoteric by nature (at *least not anymore),* but certain signs, passwords and handshakes given to the candidate during their initiation, are in fact, esoteric, in the sense that they are hidden from the general public.

Today, in the twenty-first century, such topics are readily available at bookstores across the country, and numerous mainsteam publishers offer beginners guides and coffee-table volumes on many of these subjects, intended for mass appeal. Books like *"The Secret"* have turned previously arcane topics into household knowledge. All that being the case, however, it isn't to say that there still aren't buried secrets to uncover, ancient wisdom being ignored and forgotten mysteries to be explored. In fact, it is often that we are only able to further our own studies by standing on the shoulders of these disappearing giants.

Lamp of Trismegistus is doing its part to help preserve humanity's esoteric history by making some of these classics available to those students who are seeking to unearth the knowledge of these ancient colossi.

So, be sure to check other titles from our *Esoteric Classics* series, as well as our *Occult Fiction, Theosophical Classics, Foundations of Freemasonry Series, Supernatural Fiction, Paranormal Research Series, Studies in Buddhism* and our *Christian Apocrypha Series.* You can also download the audio versions of most of these titles from Amazon, Apple or Audible, for learning on the go.

THE ORIGIN OF EVIL
by H.P. Blavatsky

THE problem of the origin of evil can be philosophically approached only if the archaic Indian formula is taken as the basis of the argument. Ancient wisdom alone solves the presence of the universal fiend in a satisfactory way. It attributes the birth of Kosmos and the evolution of life to the breaking asunder of the primordial, manifested UNITY, into plurality, or the great illusion of form. HOMOGENEITY having transformed itself into Heterogeneity, contrasts have naturally been created; hence sprang what we call EVIL, which thenceforward reigned supreme in this "Vale of Tears."

Materialistic Western philosophy (so misnamed) has not failed to profit by this grand metaphysical tenet. Even physical Science, with Chemistry at its head, has turned its attention of late to the first proposition, and directs its efforts toward proving on irrefutable data the homogeneity of primordial matter. But now steps in materialistic Pessimism, a teaching which is neither philosophy nor science, but only a deluge of meaningless words. Pessimism, in its latest development, having ceased to be pantheistic, having wedded itself to materialism, prepares to make capital out of the old Indian formula. But the atheistic pessimist soars no higher than the terrestrial homogeneous plasm of the Darwinists. For him the *ultima Thule is* earth and matter, and he sees, beyond the *prima materia,* only an ugly void, an empty nothingness. Some of the pessimists attempt to poetize their idea after the manner of the whitened sepulchres, or the Mexican corpses, whose ghastly cheeks and lips are thickly covered with rouge. The decay of matter pierces through the mask of seeming life, all efforts to the contrary notwithstanding.

Materialism patronizes Indian metaphor and imagery now. In a new work upon the subject by Dr. Mainländer, "*Pessimism and Progress,*" one learns that Indian Pantheism and German Pessimism are *identical;* and that it is the breaking up of homogeneous matter into heterogeneous material, the transition from uniformity to multiformity, which resulted in so unhappy a universe. Saith Pessimism:

This [transition] is precisely the original mistake, the *primordial sin,* which the whole creation has now to expiate by heavy suffering; it is just *that sin,* which, having launched into existence all that lives, plunged it thereby into the abysmal depths of evil and misery, to escape from which there is but one means possible, *i.e.,* by putting *an end to being itself.*

This interpretation of the Eastern formula, attributing to it the first idea of escaping the misery of life by "putting an end to being"--whether that being is viewed as applicable to the whole Kosmos, or only to individual life--is a gross misconception. The Eastern pantheist, whose philosophy teaches him to discriminate between Being or ESSE and conditioned existence, would hardly indulge in so absurd an idea as the postulation of such an alternative. He knows he can put an end to *form* alone, not to *being*-- and that only on this plane of terrestrial illusion. True, he knows that by killing out in himself *Tanha* (the unsatisfied desire for existence, or the *"will* to live")--he will thus gradually escape the curse of rebirth and *conditioned* existence. But he knows also that he cannot kill, or "put an end," even to his own little life except as a personality, which after all is but a change of dress. And believing but in One Reality, which is eternal *Be-ness,* the *"causeless* CAUSE" from which he has exiled himself into a world of forms, he regards the temporary and progressing manifestations of it in the state of Mâyâ (change or illusion), as the greatest evil, truly; but at the same time as a process in nature, as unavoidable as are the pangs of birth. It is the only means by which he can pass from limited and conditioned lives of sorrow into eternal life, or into that absolute "Be-ness," which is so graphically expressed in the Sanskrit word *sat*.

The "pessimism" of the Hindu or Buddhist pantheist is metaphysical, abstruse, and philosophical. The idea that matter and its Protean manifestations are the source and origin of universal evil and sorrow is a very old one, though Gautama Buddha was the first to give it its definite expression. But the great Indian Reformer assuredly never meant to make of it a handle for the modern pessimist to get hold of, or a peg for the materialist to hang his distorted and pernicious tenets upon!

The Sage and Philosopher, who sacrificed himself for Humanity *by living for it, in order to save it,* by teaching men to see in the sensuous existence of matter misery alone, had never in his deep philosophical mind any idea of offering a premium for suicide; his efforts were to release mankind from too strong an attachment to life, which is the chief cause of Selfishness--hence the creator of mutual pain and suffering. In his personal case, Buddha left us an example of fortitude to follow; in living, not in running away from life. His doctrine shows evil immanent, *not in matter,* which is eternal, but in the illusions created by it: through the changes and transformations of matter generating life--because these changes are conditioned and such life is ephemeral. At the same time those evils are shown to be not only unavoidable, but necessary. For if we would discern good from evil, light from darkness, and appreciate the former, we can do so only through the contrasts between the two. While Buddha's philosophy points, in its dead-letter meaning, only to the dark side of things on this illusive plane; its esotericism, the hidden soul of it, draws the veil aside and reveals to the Arhat all the glories of LIFE ETERNAL in *all the Homogeneousness of Consciousness and Being.* Another absurdity, no doubt, in the eyes of materialistic science and even modern Idealism, yet a *fact* to the Sage and esoteric pantheist.

Nevertheless, the root idea that evil is born and generated by the ever increasing complications of the homogeneous material, which enters into form and differentiates more and more as that form becomes physically more perfect, has an esoteric side to it which seems to have never occurred to the modern pessimist. Its dead-letter aspect, however, became the subject of speculation with every ancient thinking nation. Even in India the primitive thought, underlying the formula already cited, has been disfigured by Sectarianism, and has led to the ritualistic, purely dogmatic observances of the *Hatha Yogis,* in contradistinction to the philosophical Vedantic *Raja Yoga.* Pagan and Christian exoteric speculation, and even mediæval monastic asceticism, have extracted all they could from the originally noble idea, and made it subservient to their narrow-minded sectarian views. Their false conceptions of matter have led the Christians from the earliest day to identify woman with Evil and matter--notwithstanding the worship paid by the Roman Catholic Church to the Virgin.

But the latest application of the misunderstood Indian formula by the pessimists in Germany is quite original, and rather unexpected, as we shall see. To draw any analogy between a highly metaphysical teaching, and Darwin's theory of physical evolution would, in itself, seem rather a hopeless task. The more so as the theory of natural selection does not preach any conceivable extermination of *being,* but, on the contrary, a continuous and ever increasing development of *life.* Nevertheless, German ingenuity has contrived, by means of scientific paradoxes and much sophistry, to give it a semblance of philosophical truth. The old Indian tenet itself has not escaped litigation at the hands of modem pessimism. The happy discoverer of the theory, that the origin of evil dates from the protoplasmic Amoeba, which divided itself for procreation, and thus lost its immaculate homogeneity, has laid claim to the Aryan archaic formula in his new volume. While extolling its philosophy and the depth of ancient conceptions, he declares that it ought to be viewed "as the most profound truth *precogitated* and *robbed* by the ancient sages from modern thought"!

It thus follows that the deeply religious pantheism of the Hindu and Buddhist philosopher, and the occasional vagaries of the pessimistic materialist, are placed on the same level and identified by "modern thought." The impassable chasm between the two is ignored. It matters little, it seems, that the pantheist, recognizing no reality in the manifested Kosmos, and regarding it as a simple illusion of his senses, has to view his own existence also as only a bundle of illusions. When, therefore, he speaks of the means of escaping from the sufferings of objective life, his view of those sufferings, and his motive for putting an end to existence are entirely different from those of the pessimistic materialist. For him, pain as well as sorrow are illusions, due to attachment to this life, and ignorance. Therefore he strives after eternal, changeless life, and absolute consciousness in the state of Nirvana; whereas the European pessimist, taking the "evils" of life as *realities,* aspires - when he has the time to aspire after anything except those said mundane *realities,* - to annihilation of "being," as he expresses it. For the philosopher there is but one real life, *Nirvanic bliss,* which is a state differing in kind, not in degree only, from that of any of the planes of consciousness in the manifested universe. The pessimist calls "Nirvana" superstition, and explains it as "cessation of life," life for him beginning and ending on earth. The former ignores in his spiritual aspirations even the integral homogeneous unit, of which the German pessimist now makes such capital. He knows of, and believes in only the direct cause of that unit, eternal and *ever living, because the* ONE *uncreated,* or rather not evoluted. Hence all his efforts are directed toward the speediest reunion possible with, and return to his *pre*-primordial condition, after his pilgrimage through this illusive series of visionary lives, with their unreal phantasmagoria of sensuous perceptions.

Such pantheism can be qualified as "pessimistic" only by a believer in a personal Providence; by one who contrasts its negation of the reality of anything "created"--*i.e.,* conditioned and limited--with his own blind unphilosophical faith. The Oriental mind does not busy itself with extracting evil from every radical law and manifestation of life, and multiplying every phenomenal quantity by the units of very often imaginary evils: the Eastern pantheist simply submits to the inevitable, and tries to blot out from his path in life as many "descents into rebirth" as he can, by avoiding the creation of new *karmic* causes. The Buddhist philosopher knows that the duration of the series of lives of every human being--unless he reaches Nirvana "artificially" ("takes the kingdom of God by violence," in Kabalistic parlance)--is given, allegorically in the *forty-nine* days passed by Gautama the Buddha under the Bo-tree. And the Hindu sage is aware, in his turn, that he has to light the *first,* and extinguish the *forty-ninth fire*[This is an esoteric tenet, and the general reader will not make much out of it. But the Theosophist who has read *Esoteric Buddhism* may compute the 7 by 7 of the *forty-nine* "days" and the *forty-nine* "fires," and understand that the allegory refers esoterically to the seven human consecutive root-races with their seven subdivisions. Every monad is born in the first and obtains deliverance in the last seventh race. Only a "Buddha" is shown reaching it during the course of one life.] before he reaches his final deliverance. Knowing this, both sage and philosopher wait patiently for the natural hour of deliverance; whereas their unlucky copyist, the European pessimist, is ever ready to commit, as to preach, suicide. Ignorant of the numberless heads of the hydra of existences, he is incapable of feeling the same philosophical scorn for life as he does for death, and of, thereby, following the wise example given him by his Oriental brother.

Thus, philosophic pantheism is very different from modern pessimism. The first is based upon the correct understanding of the mysteries of being; the latter is in reality only one more system of evil added by unhealthy fancy to the already large sum of real social evils. In sober truth it is no philosophy, but simply a systematic slander of life and being; the bilious utterances of a dyspeptic or an incurable hypochondriac. No parallel can ever be attempted between the two systems of thought.

The seeds of evil and sorrow were indeed the earliest result and consequence of the heterogeneity of the manifested universe. Still they are but an illusion produced by the law of contrasts, which, as described, is a fundamental law in nature. Neither good nor evil would exist were it not for the light they mutually throw on each other. *Being*, under whatever form, having been observed from the World's creation to offer these contrasts, and evil predominating in the universe owing to *Ego*-ship or selfishness, the rich Oriental metaphor has pointed to existence as expiating the mistake of nature; and the human soul *(psüche)*, was henceforth regarded as the scapegoat and victim of *unconscious* OVERSOUL. But it is not to Pessimism, but to Wisdom that it gave birth.

Ignorance alone is the willing martyr, but knowledge is the master of natural pessimism. Gradually, and by the process of heredity or *atavism,* the latter became innate in man. It is always present in us, howsoever latent and silent its voice in the beginning. Amid the early joys of existence, when we are still full of the vital energies of youth, we are yet apt, each of us, at the first pang of sorrow, after a failure, or at the sudden appearance of a black cloud, to accuse *life* of it; to feel *life* a burden, and often curse our being. This shows pessimism in our blood, but at the same time the presence of the fruits of ignorance. As mankind multiplies, and with it suffering - which is the natural result of an increasing number of units that generate it - sorrow and pain are intensified. We live in an atmosphere of gloom and despair, but this is because our eyes are downcast and riveted to the earth, with all its physical and grossly material manifestations. If, instead of that, man, proceeding on his life-journey looked--not heavenward, which is but a figure of speech--but *within himself* and centered his point of observation on the *inner* man, he would soon escape from the coils of the great serpent of illusion. From the cradle to the grave, his life would then become supportable and worth living, even in its worst phases.

Pessimism - that chronic suspicion of lurking evil everywhere - is thus of a two-fold nature, and brings fruits of two kinds. It is a natural characteristic in physical man, and becomes a curse only to the ignorant. It is a boon to the spiritual, inasmuch as it makes the latter turn into the right path, and brings him to the discovery of another as fundamental a truth; namely, that all in this world is only *preparatory* because transitory. It is like a chink in the dark prison walls of earth-life, through which breaks in a ray of light from the eternal home, which, illuminating the *inner* senses, whispers to the prisoner in his shell of clay of the origin and the dual mystery of our being. At the same time, it is a tacit proof of the presence in man of that *which knows, without being told, viz:*--that there is another and a better life, once that the curse of earth-lives is lived through.

This explanation of the problem and origin of evil being, as already said, of an entirely metaphysical character, has nothing to do with physical laws. Belonging as it does altogether to the spiritual part of man, to dabble with it superficially is, therefore, far more dangerous than to remain ignorant of it. For, as it lies at the very root of Gautama Buddha's ethics, and since it has now fallen into the hands of the modern Philistines of materialism, to confuse the two systems of "pessimistic" thought can lead but to mental suicide, if it does not lead to worse.

Eastern wisdom teaches that spirit has to pass through the ordeal of incarnation and life, and be baptised with matter before it can reach experience and knowledge. After which only it receives the baptism of soul, or self-consciousness, and may return to its original condition of a god, *plus* experience, ending with omniscience. In other words, it can return to the original state of the homogeneity of primordial essence only through the addition of the fruitage of Karma, which alone is able to create an absolute *conscious* deity, removed but one degree from the absolute ALL.

Even according to the letter of the Bible, evil must have existed before Adam and Eve, who, therefore, are innocent of the slander of the original sin had there been no evil or sin before them, there could exist neither tempting Serpent nor a Tree of Knowledge of *good and evil* in Eden. The characteristics of that apple-tree are shown in the verse when the couple had tasted of its fruit: "The eyes of them both were opened, and *they knew*" many things besides knowing they were naked. Too much knowledge about things of matter is thus rightly shown an evil.

But so it is, and it is our duty to examine and combat the new pernicious theory. Hitherto, pessimism was kept in the regions of philosophy and metaphysics, and showed no pretensions to intrude into the domain of purely physical science, such as Darwinism. The theory of evolution has become almost universal now, and there is no school (save the Sunday and missionary schools) where it is not taught, with more or less modifications from the original programme. On the other hand, there is no other teaching more abused and taken advantage of than evolution, especially by the application of its fundamental laws to the solution of the most compound and abstract problems of man's many-sided existence. There, where psychology and even philosophy "fear to tread," materialistic biology applies its sledge-hammer of superficial analogies and prejudged conclusions. Worse than all, claiming man to be only a higher animal, it maintains this right as undeniably pertaining to the domain of the science of evolution. Paradoxes in those "domains" do not rain now, they pour. As "man is the measure of all things," therefore is man measured and analysed by the animal. One German materialist claims spiritual and psychic evolution as the lawful property of physiology and biology; the mysteries of embryology and zoology alone, it is said, being capable of solving those of consciousness in man and the origin of his soul [Haeckel.] Another finds justification for suicide in the example of animals, who, when tired of living, put an end to existence by starvation [Leo Bach.]

Hitherto pessimism, notwithstanding the abundance and brilliancy of its paradoxes, had a weak point - namely, the absence of any real and evident basis for it to rest upon. Its followers had no living, guiding thought to serve them as a beacon and help them to steer clear of the sandbanks of life--real and imaginary--so profusely sown by themselves in the shape of denunciations against life and being. All they could do was to rely upon their representatives, who occupied their time very ingeniously if not profitably, in tacking the many and various evils of life to the metaphysical propositions of great German thinkers, like Schopenhauer and Hartmann, as small boys tack on coloured tails to the kites of their elders and rejoice at seeing them launched in the air. But now the programme will be changed. The pessimists have found something more solid and authoritative, if less philosophical, to tack their jeremiads and dirges to, than the metaphysical *kites* of Schopenhauer. The day when they agreed with the views of this philosopher, which pointed at the Universal WILL as the perpetrator of all the World-evil, is gone to return no more. Nor will they be any better satisfied with the hazy "Unconscious" of von Hartmann. They have been seeking diligently for a more congenial and less metaphysical soil to build their pessimistic *philosophy* upon, and they have been rewarded with success, now that the cause of Universal Suffering has been discovered by them in the fundamental laws of physical development. Evil will no longer be allied with the misty and uncertain Phantom called "WILL," but with an actual and obvious fact: the pessimists will henceforth be towed by the Evolutionists.

The basic argument of their representative has been given in the opening sentence of this article. The Universe and all on it appeared in consequence of the "breaking asunder of UNITY into *Plurality.*" This rather dim rendering of the Indian formula is not made to refer, as I have shown, in the mind of the pessimist, to the one Unity, to the Vedantin abstraction - -Parabrahm: otherwise, I should not certainly have used the words "breaking up." Nor does it concern itself much with Mulaprakrti, or the "Veil" of Parabrahm; nor even with the first manifested primordial matter, except inferentially, as follows from Dr. Mainländer's exposition, but chiefly with the terrestrial *protoplasm*. Spirit or deity is entirely ignored in this case; evidently because of the necessity for showing the whole as "the lawful domain of physical Science."

In short, the time-honoured formula is claimed to have its basis and to find its justification in the theory that from "a few, perhaps one, single form of the very simplest nature" (Darwin), "all the different animals and plants living to-day, and all the organisms that have ever lived on the earth," have gradually developed. It is this axiom of Science, we are told, which justifies and demonstrates the Hindu philosophical tenet. What is this axiom? Why, it is this: Science teaches that the series of transformations through which the seed is made to pass--the seed that grows into a tree, or becomes an ovum, or that which develops into an animal--consists in every case in nothing but the passage of the fabric of that seed, from the homogeneous into the heterogeneous or compound form. This is then the scientific verity which checks the Indian formula by that of the Evolutionists, identifies both, and thus exalts ancient wisdom by recognizing it worthy of modern materialistic thought.

This philosophical formula is not simply corroborated by the individual growth and development of isolated species, explains our pessimist; but it is demonstrated in general as in detail. It is shown justified in the evolution and growth of the Universe as well as in that of our planet. In short, the birth, growth and development of the whole organic world in its integral totality, are there to demonstrate ancient wisdom. From the universals down to the particulars, the organic world is discovered to be subject to the same law of ever increasing elaboration, of the transition from unity to plurality as "the fundamental formula of the evolution of life." Even the growth of nations, of social life, public institutions, the development of the languages, arts and sciences, - all this follows inevitably and fatally the all-embracing law of "the breaking asunder of unity into plurality, and the passage of the homogeneous into multiformity."

But while following Indian wisdom, our author exaggerates this fundamental law in his own way, and distorts it. He brings this law to bear even on the historical destinies of mankind. He makes these destinies subservient to, and a proof of, the correctness of the Indian conception.

He maintains that humanity as an integral whole, in proportion as it develops and progresses in its evolution, and separates in its parts - each becoming a distinct and independent branch of the unit - drifts more and more away from its original healthy, harmonious unity. The complications of social establishment, social relations, as those of individuality, all lead to the weakening of the vital power, the relaxation of the energy of feeling, and to the destruction of that integral unity, without which no inner harmony is possible. The absence of that harmony generates an inner discord which becomes the cause of the greatest mental misery. Evil has its roots in the very nature of the evolution of life and its complications. Every one of its steps forward is at the same time a step taken toward the dissolution of its energy, and leads to passive apathy. Such is the inevitable result, he says, of every progressive complication of life; because evolution or development is a transition from the homogeneous to the heterogeneous, a scattering of the whole into the many, etc., etc. The terrible law is universal and applies to all creation, from the infinitesimally small up to man for, as he says, it is a fundamental law of nature.

Now, it is just in this one-sided view of physical nature, which the German author accepts without one single thought as to its spiritual and psychic aspect, that his school is doomed to certain failure. It is not a question whether the said law of differentiation and its fatal consequences may or may not apply, in certain cases, to the growth and development of the animal species, and even of man;

but simply, since it is the basis and main support of the whole new theory of the pessimistic school, whether it is really a *universal* and fundamental law? We want to know whether this basic formula of evolution embraces the whole process of development and growth in its entirety; and whether, indeed, it is within the domain of physical science or not. If it is "nothing else than the transition from the homogeneous state to the heterogeneous," as says Mainländer, then it remains to be proved that the given process "produces that complicated combination of tissues and organs which forms and completes the perfect animal and plant."

As remarked already by some critics on "Pessimism and Progress," the German pessimist does not doubt it for one moment. His supposed discovery and teaching "rest wholly on his certitude that development and the fundamental law of the complicated process of organization represent but one thing: the transformation of unity into plurality." Hence the identification of the process with dissolution and decay, and the weakening of all the forces and energies. Mainländer would be right in his analogies were this law of the differentiation of the homogeneous into the heterogeneous to really represent the fundamental law of the evolution of life. But the idea is quite erroneous - metaphysically as well as physically. Evolution does not proceed in a straight line; *no more* than any other process in nature, but journeys on *cyclically,* as does all the rest. The cyclic serpents swallow their tails like the Serpent of Eternity. And it is in this that the Indian formula, which is a Secret Doctrine teaching, is indeed corroborated by the natural Sciences, and especially by biology.

This is what we read in the "*Scientific Letters*" by an anonymous Russian author and critic:

In the evolution of isolated individuals, in the evolution of the organic world, in that of the Universe, as in the growth and development of our planet--in short wherever any of the processes of progressive complexity take place, there we find, apart from the transition from unity to plurality, and homogeneity to heterogeneity, *a converse transformation--the transition front plurality to unity, from the heterogeneous to the homogeneous.* . . . Minute observation of the given process of progressive complexity has shown, that what takes place in it is not alone the separation of parts, but also their mutual absorption. . . . While one portion of the cells merge into each other and unite into one uniform whole. forming muscular fibres, muscular tissue, others are absorbed in the bone and nerve tissues, etc., etc. The same take place in the formation of plants. . . .

In this case material nature repeats the law that acts in the evolution of the psychic and the spiritual: both descend but to reascend and merge at the starting-point. *The homogeneous formative mass or element differentiated in its parts, is gradually transformed into the heterogeneous; then, merging those parts into a harmonious whole, it recommences a converse process, or reinvolution, and returns as gradually into its primitive or primordial state.*

Nor does Pessimism find any better support in pure Materialism, as hitherto the latter has been tinged with a decidedly optimistic bias. Its leading advocates have, indeed, never hesitated to sneer at the theological adoration of the "glory of God and all his works." Büchner flings a taunt at the pantheist who sees in so "mad and bad" a world the manifestation of the Absolute. But, on the whole, the materialists admit a balance of good over evil, perhaps as a buffer against any "superstitious" tendency to look out and hope for a better one. Narrow as is their outlook, and limited as is their spiritual horizon, they yet see no cause to despair of the drift of things in general. The *pantheistic* pessimists, however, have never ceased to urge that a despair of conscious being is the only legitimate outcome of atheistic negation. This opinion is, of course, axiomatic, or ought to be so. If "in this life only is there hope," the tragedy of life is absolutely without any *raison d'être* and a perpetuation of the drama is as foolish as it is futile.

The fact that the conclusions of pessimism have been at last assimilated by a certain class of atheistic writers, is a striking feature of the day, and another sign of the times. It illustrates the truism that the void created by modern scientific negation cannot and never can be filled by the cold prospects offered as a *solatium to* optimists. The Comtean "enthusiasm of Humanity" is a poor thing enough with annihilation of the Race to ensue "as the solar fires die slowly out"--if, indeed, *they do die* at all--to please physical science at the computed time. If all present sorrow and suffering, the fierce struggle for existence and all its attendant horrors, go for nothing in the long run, if MAN is a mere ephemeron, the sport of blind forces, why assist in the perpetuation of the farce? The "ceaseless grind of matter, force and law," will but hurry the swarming human millions into eternal oblivion, and ultimately leave no trace or memory of the past, when things return to the nebulosity of the fire-mist, whence they emerged. Terrestrial life is no object in itself. It is overcast with gloom and misery. It does not seem strange, then, that the Soul-blind negationist should prefer the pessimism of Schopenhauer to the baseless optimism of Strauss and his followers, which, in the face of their teachings, reminds one of the animal spirits of a young donkey, after a good meal of thistles.

One thing is, however, clear: the absolute necessity for some solution, which embraces the facts of existence on an optimistic basis. Modern Society is permeated with an increasing cynicism and honeycombed with disgust of life. This is the result of an utter ignorance of the operations of Karma and the nature of Soul evolution. It is from a mistaken allegiance to the dogmas of a mechanical and largely spurious theory of Evolution, that Pessimism has risen to such undue importance. Once the basis of the Great Law is grasped -and what philosophy can furnish better means for such a grasp and final solution, than the esoteric doctrine of the great Indian Sages? - there remains no possible *locus standi* for the recent amendments to the Schopenhauerian system of thought or the metaphysical subtleties, woven by the "philosopher of the Unconscious." The reasonableness of *conscious* Existence can be proved only by the study of the primeval--now esoteric--philosophy. And it says "there is neither death nor life, for both are illusions; being (or *be-ness) is* the only reality." This paradox was repeated thousands of ages later by one of the greatest physiologists that ever lived. "Life is Death," said Claude Bernard. The organism lives because its parts are ever dying. The survival of the fittest is surely based on this truism. The life of the superior whole requires the death of the inferior, the death of the parts depending on and being subservient to it. And, as life is death, so death is life, and the whole great cycle of lives form but ONE EXISTENCE--*the worst day of which is on our planet.*

He who KNOWS will make the best of it. For there is a dawn for every being, when once freed from illusion and ignorance by Knowledge; and he will at last proclaim in truth *and all Consciousness* to Mahamâyâ:

BROKEN THY HOUSE IS, AND THE RIDGE-POLE
SPLIT! DELUSION FASHIONED IT!
SAFE PASS I THENCE--DELIVERANCE TO OBTAIN. . . .

STRAY THOUGHTS ON DEATH AND SATAN

TO THE EDITOR OF THE THEOSOPHIST

Madam,—Since you have published a posthumous letter of my Master and beloved friend, the late Éliphas Lévi, I think it would be agreeable to you to publish, if judged suitable, a few extracts of the many manuscripts in my possession, written expressly for, and given to, me by my ever-regretted MASTER.

To begin, I send you—"Stray Thoughts on Death and Satan" from his pen.

I cannot close this letter without expressing the deep indignation aroused in me by the base diatribes published in the *London Spiritualist* against your Society and its members. Every honest heart is irritated at such unfair treatment, especially when proceeding from a man of honour as Mr. Harrison (Editor of the *Spiritualist*) who admits in his journal anonymous contributions that are tantamount to libels.

With the utmost respect,
I remain, Madam,
Yours Devotedly,
BARON J. SPADALIERI
Marseilles, July 29, 1881

Editor's Note.—It is with feelings of sincere gratitude that we thank Baron Spadalieri for his most valuable contribution. The late Éliphas Lévi was the most learned Kabalist and Occultist of our age, in Europe, and every thing from his pen is precious to us, in so far as it helps us to compare notes with the Eastern Occult doctrines and, by the light thrown upon both, to prove to the world of Spiritualists and Mystics, that the two systems—the Eastern-Aryan, and the Western or the Chaldeo-Jewish Kabala—are one in their principal metaphysical tenets. Only, while the Eastern Occultists have never lost the key to their esotericism, and are daily verifying and elaborating their doctrines by personal experiments, and by the additional light of modern science, the Western or Jewish Kabalists, besides having been misled for centuries by the introduction of foreign elements in it such as Christian dogmas, dead-letter interpretations of the Bible &c., have most undeniably lost the true key to the esoteric meaning of Simeon Ben Jochai's Kabala, and are trying to make up for the loss, by interpretations emanating from the depths of their imagination and inner consciousness. Such is evidently the case with J. K., the self-styled London "Adept," whose anonymous and powerless vilifications of the Theosophical Society and its members are pertinently regarded by Baron Spadalieri as "tantamount to libels." But we have to be charitable. That poor descendant of the Biblical *Levites*—as we know him to be—in his pigmy efforts to upset the Theosophists, has most evidently fractured his brain against one of his own "occult" sentences. There is one especially in the *Spiritualist* (July 22), to which the attention of the mystically inclined is drawn further down as this paragraph is most probably the cause of the sad accident which befell so handsome a head. Be it as it may, but it now disables the illustrious J.K. from communicating "scientifically his knowledge" and forces him at the same time to remain, as he expresses it, "in an incommunicable ecstatic state." For it is in no other "state" that our great modern adept, the literary man of such a "calibre"[1] that to

---

[1] "To accuse a *literary man of my calibre* of ignorance, is as amusing a mistake as it would have been to charge Porson of ignorance of Greek," he writes in the *Spiritualist* of July 8. . . ."The occult is my special subject, and . . . *there is but little . . . that I do not know,*" he adds. Now, the above sentence settles the question at rest with us. Not only an "*adept*" but no layman or profane of the most widely recognized intellect and ability, would have ever *dared*, under the penalty of being henceforth and for ever regarded as the most ridiculously conceited

suspect him of "ignorance" becomes equal, in audacity, to throwing suspicion upon the virtue of Caesar's wife—could possibly have written the following lines, intended by him, we believe, as a *lucid* and clear exposition of his own psycho-Kabalistic lore as juxtaposed to the "hard words," "outlandish verbiage," "moral and philosophical platitudes," and "jaw-breakers" of "the learned Theosophists."

These are the "gems of occult wisdom" of the illustrious Jewish Kabalist who, like a bashful violet, hides his occult learning under two modest initials.

"In every human creature there lies latent in the involitional part of the being a sufficient quantity of the omniscient, the absolute. To induce the latent absolute, which *is* the involitional part of our volitional conscious being, to become manifest, it is essential that the volitional part of our being should become latent. After the preparatory purification from acquired depravities, a kind of introversion has to take place; the involitional has to become volitional, by the volitional becoming involitional. When the conscious becomes semi-unconscious, the, to us, formerly unconscious becomes fully conscious. The particle of the omniscient that is within us, the vital and growing, sleepless, involitional, occult or female principle being allowed to express itself in the volitional, mental, manifest, or masculine part of the human being, while the latter remains in a state of perfect passivity, the two formerly dissevered parts become re-united as one holy (wholly)

---

of—Æsopus' heroes—to use such a sentence when speaking of himself! So stupidly arrogant, and cowardly impertinent has he shown himself behind the shield of his initials to far better and more worthy men than himself, in his transparent attacks upon them in the above-named *Spiritualist*—that it is the first and certainly the last time that we do him the honour of noticing him in these columns. Our journal has a nobler task, we trust, than to be polemizing with those, whom in vulgar parlance the world generally terms—*bullies*—ED. THEOS.

perfect being, and then the divine manifestation is inevitable." Very luckily, J.K. gives us himself the key to this grandiloquent gush: "necessarily" he adds, "this is only safely practicable while living in uncompromisingly firm purity, for otherwise there is danger of *unbalancement—insanity*, or a questionable form of *mediumship*."

The italics are ours. Evidently with our *immaculate* "adept" the "involitional, occult or *female* principle" was *not* allowed to express itself in the volitional mental, manifest, or masculine part" of his being, and—behold the results!!

For the edification of our Hindu readers, who are unprogressive enough to refuse reading the lucubrations of "J.K.," or follow the mental "grand trapeze" performed by this remarkable Adept" on the columns of the *Spiritualist*, we may add that in he same article he informs his English readers that it is "Hindu mystification, acting on Western credulity" which "brought out the Theosophical Society." "Hindu philosophy" according to that great light of the nineteenth century is no "philosophy" but rather mysticism." . . . "Following the track of the mystifying and mystified Hindus they (the Theosophists) consider the four above faculties (Sidhis of Krishna) Anima, Mahima, Laghima and Garima to be the power they (we) have to strive for." "Indeed, what a ludicrous confusion of effect with cause"!

The fracture of the brain must have been serious indeed. Let us hope that timely and repeated lotions of "Witch-Hazel" or "the Universal Magic Balm" will have its good effects. Meanwhile, we turn the attention of our Hindu readers and students of Occultism to the identity of the doctrines taught by Éliphas Lévi (who, too, is contemptuously sneered at, and sent by the "Adept" to keep company with "Brothers," Yogis, and "Fakirs") in every essential and vital point with those of our Eastern initiates.

-- H.P.B.

I. DEATH

By Eliphas Levi

Death is the necessary dissolution of imperfect combinations. It is the re-absorption of the rough outline of individual life into the great work of universal life; only the perfect is immortal.

It is a bath in oblivion. It is the fountain of youth where on one side plunges old age, and whence on the other issues infancy.[2]

Death is the transfiguration of the living; corpses are but the dead leaves of the Tree of Life which will still have all its leaves in the spring. The resurrection of men resembles eternally these leaves.

Perishable forms are conditioned by immortal types.

All who have lived upon earth, live there still in new exemplars of their types, but the souls which have surpassed their type receive elsewhere a new form based upon a more perfect type, as they mount ever on the ladder of worlds;[3] the bad exemplars are broken, and their matter returned into the general mass.[4]

Our souls are as it were a music, of which our bodies are the instruments. The music exists without the instruments, but it cannot

---

[2] Rebirth of the *Ego* after death, The Eastern, and especially Buddhistic doctrine of the evolution of the new, out of the old *Ego*.—ED. THEOS.

[3] From one *loka* to the other; from a positive world of causes and activity, to a negative world of effects and passivity.—ED. THEOS.

[4] Into Cosmic matter, when they necessarily lose their self-consciousness or individuality or are annihilated, as the Eastern Kabalists say.—ED. THEOS.

make itself heard without a material intermediary; the immaterial can neither be conceived nor grasped.

Man in his present existence only retains certain predispositions from his past existences.

Evocations of the dead are but condensations of memory, the imaginary coloration of the shades. To evoke those who are no longer there, is but to cause their types to re-issue from the imagination of nature.[5]

To be in direct communication with the imagination of nature, one must be either asleep, intoxicated, in an ecstacy, cataleptic, or mad.

The eternal memory preserves only the imperishable; all that passes in Time belongs of right to oblivion.

The preservation of corpses is a violation of the laws of nature; it is an outrage on the modesty of death, which hides the works of destruction, as we should hide those of reproduction. Preserving corpses is to create phantoms in the imagination of the earth;[6] the spectres of the night-mare, of hallucination, and fear, are but the wandering photographs of preserved corpses. It is these preserved or imperfectly destroyed corpses, which spread, amid the living, plague, cholera, contagious diseases, sadness, scepticism and disgust

---

[5] To ardently desire to see a dead person is to *evoke* the images of that person, to call it forth from the astral light or ether wherein rest photographed the images of the *Past*. That is what is being partially done in the *seance-rooms*. The Spiritualists are unconscious NECROMANCERS.—ED. THEOS.

[6] To intensify these images in the astral or sidereal light.—ED. THEOS.

of life.⁷ Death is exhaled by death. The cemeteries poison the atmosphere of towns, and the miasma of corpses blight the children even in the bosoms of their mothers.

Near Jerusalem in the Valley of Gehenna a perpetual fire was maintained for the combustion of filth and the carcasses of animals, and it is to this eternal fire that Jesus alluded when he says that the wicked shall be cast into *Gehenna*; signifying that dead souls will be treated as corpses.

The Talmud says that the souls of those who have not believed in immortality will not become immortal. It is faith only which gives personal immortality;⁸ science and reason can only affirm the general immortality.

The mortal sin is the suicide of the soul. This suicide would occur if the man devoted himself to evil with the full strength of his mind, with a perfect knowledge of good and evil, and an entire liberty of action which seems impossible in practice, but which is possible in theory, because the essence of an independent personality is an unconditioned liberty. The divinity imposes nothing upon man, not even existence. Man has a right to withdraw himself even from the divine goodness, and the dogma of eternal hell is only the assertion of eternal free-will.

---

⁷ People begin intuitionally to realize the great truth, and societies for burning bodies and *crematories* are now started in many places in Europe.—ED. THEOS.

⁸ Faith and *will power*. Immortality is conditional, as we have ever stated. It is the reward of the pure and good. The wicked man, the material sensualist only survives. He who appreciates but physical pleasures will not and *cannot* live in the hereafter as a self-conscious Entity.—ED. THEOS.

God precipitates no one into hell. It is men who can go there freely, definitively and by their own choice.

Those who are in hell, that is to say, amid the gloom of evil[9] and the sufferings of the necessary punishment, without having absolutely so willed it, are called to emerge from it. This hell is for them only a purgatory. The damned completely, absolutely and without respite, is Satan who is not a rational existence, but a necessary hypothesis.

Satan is the last word of the creation. He is the end infinitely emancipated. He willed to be like God of which he is the opposite. God is the hypothesis necessary to reason, Satan the hypothesis necessary to unreason asserting itself as free-will.

To be immortal in good, one must identify oneself with God; to be immortal in evil, with Satan. These are the two poles of the world of souls; between these two poles vegetate and die without remembrance the useless portion of mankind.

Editor's Note.—This may seem incomprehensible to the average reader, for it is one of the most abstruse of the tenets of Occult doctrine. Nature is dual: there is a physical and material side, as there is a spiritual and moral side to it; and, there is both good and evil in it, the latter the necessary shadow to its light. To force oneself upon the current of immortality, or rather to secure for oneself an endless series of rebirths as conscious individualities—says the Book of

---

[9] That is to say, they are reborn in a "lower world" which is neither "Hell" nor any theological purgatory, but a world of nearly absolute *matter* and one preceding the last one in the "circle of necessity" from which "there is no redemption, for there reigns *absolute* spiritual darkness." (Book of Khiu-te.)—ED. THEOS.

Khiu-te Vol. XXXI, one must become a co-worker with nature, either for *good* or for *bad*, in her work of creation and reproduction, or in that of destruction. It is but the useless drones, which she gets rid of, violently ejecting and making them perish by the millions as self-conscious entities. Thus, while the good and the pure strive to reach *Nipang* (*nirvana* or that state of *absolute* existence and *absolute* consciousness—which, in the world of finite perceptions, is *non*-existence and *non*-consciousness)—the wicked will seek, on the contrary, a series of lives as conscious, definite existences or beings, preferring to be ever suffering under the law of retributive justice rather than give up their lives as portions of the integral, universal whole. Being well aware that they can never hope to reach the final rest in pure spirit, or *nirvana*, they cling to life in any form, rather than give up that "desire for life," or *Tanha* which causes a new aggregation of *Skandas* or individuality to be reborn. Nature is as good a mother to the cruel bird of prey as she is to the harmless dove. Mother nature will punish her child, but since he has become her co-worker for destruction she cannot eject him. There are thoroughly wicked and depraved men, yet as highly intellectual and acutely *spiritual* for evil, as those who are spiritual for good. The *Egos* of these may escape the law of final destruction or annihilation for ages to come. That is what Éliphas Lévi means by becoming "immortal in evil," through identification with Satan. "I would thou wert *cold* or *hot*," says the vision of the *Revelation* to St. John (III. 15-16). "So then because thou art, *lukewarm* and neither cold nor hot, I will spue thee out of my mouth." The *Revelation* is an absolutely *Kabalistic* book. Heat and cold are the two "poles," *i.e.*, good and evil, *spirit* and *matter*. Nature *spues* the "lukewarm" or "the useless portion of mankind" out of her mouth, *i.e.*, annihilates them. This conception that a considerable portion of mankind may after all not have immortal souls, will not be new even to European readers. Coleridge himself likened the case to that of an oak tree bearing, indeed, millions of acorns, but acorns of which under normal conditions not one in a thousand ever developed into a tree, and suggested that as the majority of the acorns failed to develop into a new living tree, so possibly the majority of men fail to develop into a new living entity after this earthly death.

II. SATAN

By Eliphas Levi

Satan is merely a type, not a real personage.

It is the type opposed to the Divine type, the necessary foil to this in our imagination. It is the factitious shadow which renders visible to us the infinite light of the Divine.

If Satan was a real personage then would there be two Gods, and the creed of the Manicheans would be a truth.

Satan is the imaginary conception of the absolute in evil; a conception necessary to the complete affirmation of the liberty of the human will, which, by the help of this imaginary absolute seems able to equilibrate the entire power even of God. It is the boldest, and perhaps, the sublimest of the dreams of human pride.

"You shall be as Gods knowing good and evil," saith the allegorical serpent in the Bible. Truly to make evil a science is to create a God of evil, and if any spirit can eternally resist God, there is no longer one God but two Gods.

To resist the Infinite, infinite force is necessary, and two infinite forces opposed to each other must neutralize each other.[10] If

---

[10] And evil being infinite and eternal. for it is coêval with matter, the logical deduction would be that there is neither God nor Devil—as personal Entities, only One Uncreated, Infinite, Immutable and Absolute Principle or Law: EVIL or DEVIL—the deeper it falls into

resistance on the part of Satan is possible the power of God no longer exists, God and the Devil destroy each other, and man remains alone; he remains alone with the phantom of his Gods, the hybrid sphynx, the winged bull, which poises in its human hand a sword of which the wavering lightnings drive the human imagination from one error to the other, and from the despotism of the light, to the despotism of the darkness.

The history of mundane misery is but the romance of the war of the Gods, a war still unfinished, while the Christian world still adores a God in the Devil, and a Devil in God.

The antagonism of powers is anarchy in Dogma. Thus to the church which affirms that the Devil exists the world replies with a terrifying logic: then God does not exist; and it is vain to seek escape from this argument to invent the supremacy of a God who would permit a Devil to bring about the damnation of men; such a permission would be a monstrosity, and would amount to complicity, and the god that could be an accomplice of the devil, cannot be God.

The Devil of Dogmas is a personification of Atheism. The Devil of Philosophy is the exaggerated ideal of human free-will. The real or physical Devil is the magnetism of evil.

Raising the Devil is but realizing for an instant this imaginary personality. This involves the exaggeration in one's self beyond

---

matter, GOOD or GOD as soon as it is purified from the latter and re-becomes again pure unalloyed Spirit or the ABSOLUTE in its everlasting, immutable Subjectivity.— ED. THEOS.

bounds of the perversity of madness by the most criminal and senseless acts.

The result of this operation is the death of the soul through madness, and often the death of the body even, lightning-struck, as it were, by a cerebral congestion.

The Devil ever importunes, but nothing ever gives in return.

St. John calls it "the Beast" (*la Bête*) because its essence is human folly (*la Bêtise humaine*).

Éliphas Lévi's *(Bonæ Memoriæ)* creed, and that of his disciples.

We believe in a God-Principle, the essence of all existence, of all good and of all justice, inseparable from nature which is its law and which reveals itself through intelligence and love.

We believe in Humanity, daughter of God, of which all the members are indissolubly connected one with the other so that all must co-operate in the salvation of each, and each in the salvation of all.

We believe that to serve the Divine essence it is necessary to serve Humanity.

We believe in the reparation of evil, and in the triumph of good in the life eternal.

FIAT

www.ingramcontent.com/pod-product-compliance
Lightning Source LLC
LaVergne TN
LVHW041502070426
835507LV00009B/773